THE TREE FOLK OF TILSON BAY

LeeAnn Meer

BALBOA.
PRESS

A DIVISION OF HAY HOUSE

Balboa Press books may be ordered through booksellers or by contacting:

Balboa Press
A Division of Hay House
1663 Liberty Drive
Bloomington, IN 47403
www.balboapress.com
1 (877) 407-4847

Because of the dynamic nature of the Internet, any web addresses or
links contained in this book may have changed since publication and
may no longer be valid. The views expressed in this work are solely those
of the author and do not necessarily reflect the views of the publisher,
and the publisher hereby disclaims any responsibility for them.

The author of this book does not dispense medical advice or prescribe the use
of any technique as a form of treatment for physical, emotional, or medical
problems without the advice of a physician, either directly or indirectly. The
intent of the author is only to offer information of a general nature to help
you in your quest for emotional and spiritual well-being. In the event you use
any of the information in this book for yourself, which is your constitutional
right, the author and the publisher assume no responsibility for your actions.

Any people depicted in stock imagery provided by Thinkstock are
models, and such images are being used for illustrative purposes only.
Certain stock imagery © Thinkstock.

Print information available on the last page.

ISBN: 978-1-5043-7462-0 (sc)
ISBN: 978-1-5043-7463-7 (e)

Balboa Press rev. date: 02/09/2016

CONTENTS

I first began writing poetry when I was a child. My family owned a cottage on Kentucky Lake, and we spent many a summer day down there. It truly was an idyllic childhood, and our times there were magical. We had no television, no phone, and for all practical purposes, no radio. We were a family of six—two boys, two girls, and a mom and dad. We created our own entertainment, inventing and playing games. One of the things we used to do on a rainy day, or in the evenings, was to write poetry. We would take turns coming up with a topic, and then everyone would write a poem on that topic. There was a time limit, so some—no, many—of the poems were ... really bad. But every now and then, someone would come up with something pretty darn clever. The fun we had, the laughter and the memories created, are still with me today. At least twenty years ago, I started writing a yearly poem to my brothers and sisters and their children. Like the poems at Kentucky Lake, they were not very good. But it became a tradition. My sister informed me one year that her four kids look forward to the poem each year! So I continue.

In 2004, I became aware of the book and movie, The Secret. There I learned about the law of attraction, the power of gratitude, positive thinking, and intentionally living your life. This led me to Hay House, where I purchased many books and hungrily read as much as I could. This knowledge changed my life and has put me on a path that is filled with happiness, joy, and positive energy. I noticed that I began to look at the world differently—and the world looked different. At this point, poems started coming out of me about the wondrous things I saw. I believe I live in paradise and am fortunate to see Mother Nature in all her glory and in four distinctly different seasons. I have come to see characters, creatures, and designs in nature everywhere I look. Whether I am looking at the clouds, the water, the shapes of trees, the icy creations of winter, or anything in nature, there are so many things to see. I am truly amazed and incredibly grateful to see what I see and to be able to write these poems. I hope you find some enjoyment in reading them.

One of my favorite spots to enjoy is my front yard and the lake. I live on beautiful Rainy Lake in northern Minnesota and am able to daily see a plethora of sights. From wildlife to trees, to flowers, to processes of nature, to dynamic seasonal changes, there is always something to see and always a different way to see it. One winter, I was amazed at how many smiles I saw in all the trees. These smiles were snow that had partially slipped off the branches, resulting in a smile. Then I noticed they were everywhere. I, of course, couldn't help but smile when looking at them. They were always there; what had changed was that now I saw them.

As I look across the bay, there are six trees with very, in my opinion, distinctive shapes. I can easily see these creatures; they each have a name, and I greet them every day. I can see their "cousins" all around the lake—so my first poem and the title of the book is The Tree Folk of Tilson Bay.

Photo by Mary Truscott

The Tree Folk of Tilson Bay

If you really look closely at something,
it doesn't matter the size.
It's amazing what you can see
right there before your eyes.

Just use your imagination
and see beyond what you know is there.
There are characters, designs, and creatures
just waiting to be seen everywhere.

As I look out of my window
across the bay, I see a group of trees.
To me they're the tree folk of Tilson Bay—
six characters I can clearly see.

These tree folk stand tall on the horizon
as if guarding this piece of the bay.
They're as familiar to me as the morning sun,
making me smile and feel grateful every day.

I find their kin all around the lake,
almost as sentinels watching over all.

They bring with them a sense of strength and awe
as they stoically and silently stand tall.

Now you can find shapes and creatures in the clouds.
The snow and ice are another good source.
The wind creates incredible designs,
but the trees, to me, have a spiritual force.

Yes, everywhere I look, nature
seems to have a magic all its own.
There is miraculous beauty in everything—
it just depends on the lens through which it is shown.

Whether it's shapes or angles of branches
or smiles in the branches made of snow,
I truly feel joy and am never alone.
I just let my imagination go.

By looking for the beauty and designs
that surround us wherever we are,
we change the way we look at things,
allowing our spirits and love to reach far.

The best part about all of this
is you get to decide which it will be.
You can look for the miracles in everything
and let your heart and soul truly see.

So as I look at these tree folk,
I want you to look around you.
Start to see this other world—
its beauty. It's miraculous. It's true.

As mentioned earlier, I live on beautiful Rainy Lake, the sixtieth largest freshwater lake in North America. It is on the Canadian border and has a beautiful golden summer and a long and cold winter. Water, in all her many forms, is a large part of our lives.

WATER

Water is a necessity of life.
Without it we wouldn't be alive.
Did you know it makes up three-quarters of us?
Literally everything needs it to survive.

Water is soothing to the soul,
to see it and hear it too.
The negative ions you get from water
are actually quite healthy for you.

I sit and watch the water in the lake—
it can mesmerize for hours on end
as it laps and flows, glistens and glows,
always playing the tune of the wind.

Water connects with all of your senses.
You can smell it in the air.
After a long winter when water was ice,
we finally start to see it everywhere.

One thing that is music to my ears
is the sound of dripping water in the spring.
It will start to pool and run and flow,
and the sounds of promised warmth will ring.

Water is part of this wonderful cycle
that circulates itself all the time.
It's nature's way of recycling life
from the land to the sea to the sky.

Yes, water is truly remarkable,
filling the needs of all life on earth.
It's a common thread that everything shares
and renews all of us, like a new birth.

RAIN

The rains that fall from the sky
are a necessity and a gift to us all.
They nourish the earth and the wildlife within,
setting up a cycle like a never-ending waterfall.

You can smell the rain before it comes
and often see it moving across the sky.
It can fall ever so gently
or in torrents that can terrify.

I've heard you can read the weather signs
from the animals, the plants, and such.
You can predict the weather—especially the rain—
by what you learn, know, and trust.

Getting out for a walk on a rainy day
can be an adventure you won't forget.
Allow yourself the luxury to explore—
the world looks quite different when wet.

Have you ever watched a puddle form?
Or seen the leaves bend under a raindrop's weight?
The color of the bark on the trees will change,
and the worms seem to come out to celebrate!

What about feeling it in your bones
or seeing signs of coming rain outside?
The cows will lie down before a rain,
and the flowers close up for the ride.

The crowning jewel of the rains that fall
comes at the end of nature's show,
with the most beautiful and colorful phenomenon—
an incredible, full-spectrum rainbow!

So enjoy the rains that fall from the sky,
as we wouldn't survive without.
After all, water is a large part of us—
something we need without a doubt.

The Gift of Snow

It snowed again here last night.
How lucky can one be?
The beauty that the snow can bring
will be enjoyed most gratefully.

The snowflakes come in incredible shapes,
worthy of the time to really see.
So stop when you can and go outside
and take part in nature's reality.

The crystals are multifaceted,
reflecting the light with every move.
They sparkle and shimmer like diamonds,
feeding the soul as though they were food.

The wind adds her touch to the canvas,
creating the most delightful designs.
She sculpts the landscape with drifts and furls,
a masterpiece that is truly fine.

The sun takes her turn with this work of art,
softening the edges with her warm gaze.
The creation will change day to day,
often left coated with a magnificent glaze.

This snow will melt and refreeze at night,
once again making intricate shapes.
It's like an ever-changing tapestry,
sort of like nature's own icy drapes.

So try to embrace it as the gift it is,
the snow that falls from the sky.
Enjoy each stage with the delight it deserves.
Your heart and soul will sigh.

Wind is also a big force up here. I have seen stronger winds up here than anywhere I have ever lived. I saw the wind once take a trampoline and flip it over a fifty-foot tree and into the lake. I also saw the wind take a canoe that was filled with water and blow it off a dock. It even picked up our sixteen-foot sailboat and laid it on the dock! Wind is something you have to deal with and must respect. It is also a beautiful artist! I never cease to be amazed at what the wind can create.

WIND

I have never seen the wind before.
I guess I didn't know you could.
Her effects are certainly noticed
on the water, the land, and the wood.

"But how do you see the wind?" you ask.
With her efforts everywhere, you gaze.
She seems to be invisible herself,
yet she touches everything and will amaze.

The leaves will start to wave at you.
The dust will swirl 'round and 'round.
The flowers bend, and the branches sway—
sometimes you can hear her howling sound.

You can see the wind on the water
as it races across the top.
You can feel it on your hair and skin
and can smell the rain about to pop.

In the wintertime, she's at her best,
with her canvas being the snow on the ground.
There's an ever-changing masterpiece
that never ceases to please and astound.

But to see her just all by herself,
well, it's never happened to me.
And yet there's no doubt she's there—
a great example of what you know, not see.

So in this amazing world where we live,
have faith in what you know to be.
Sometimes the best joys in life
are those we cannot really see.

The seasons are dynamic up here. They can come so quickly and so explosively. I do love and enjoy these seasonal changes every year. The springtime is amazing, as it is literally like an explosion.

EXPLOSION OF LIFE

Every year in the spring,
there's a literal explosion of life.
To me it's a thrilling experience
that fills me with awe and delight.

When winter finally loosens her grip
and the snow and ice disappear,
the explosion happens quite rapidly,
and the greening is amazing each year.

The buds start to show up on the trees
and visibly grow each day.
The pale-green color soon takes over,
and new life is simply the way.

The grass greens up amazingly fast—
you can almost watch it occur.
Just give it warmth, sunshine, and rain,
and the miracle will happen for sure.

The flowers stir after a winter's sleep
and slowly poke their heads through the ground.
The miracle of life starts to do its thing,
and nature's colors will soon abound.

The birds start to return to us—
more and more come back each day.
Their songs are a blessing to my heart.
It's amazing they find their way.

The duck return is a favorite of mine—
the incredible performance delights.
Their colors and calls are amazing to see,
and the mating dances are quite a sight.

Then all of a sudden the bugs are back,
buzzing and biting too.
They are part of the explosion of life
and, like all, connect to me and you.

Every year, this phenomenon does occur,
and somehow it is always better than last year.
It fills me with love and sheer gratitude.
Life is good on this amazing sphere.

THE SEASONS

One of the things I truly love
about living in the north woods
is the dynamic seasonal changes we have—
it's spectacular, miraculous, and good.

The springtime is quite amazing
as the explosion of life is underway.
It's an exciting time with change every day,
sort of like nature's life-filled buffet.

Summertime is also truly grand—
the time of year when everything should pause,
so we can take in the warmth and the sun
and enjoy nature in all her applause.

The takeover of life that summertime brings
is a testament to the abundance of our world.
The land is filled with life of all kinds
as though nature's wings have fully unfurled.

Then fall comes along;
it always sort of sneaks up fast.
The leaves change colors with an amazing show
and take the lead in this all-star cast.

The colors they make are breathtaking to see,
a full-spectrum rainbow they are.
The air crisps up, and the sun loses strength,
letting us know that winter is not far.

Wintertime is an amazing thing.
It can happen almost overnight.
I'm amazed that machines will even work—
yet they do—well, most of the time.

Yet winter is quite beautiful
with all the snow and the ice.
There's so much to do—even outside.
It's a beautiful, frozen paradise.

Yes, the seasonal changes are extreme,
more than any other place I've lived.
They each are incredibly beautiful
and from all angles truly a gift.

We are known up here as the "Icebox of the Nation," a moniker I never understood touting. However, we do get quite cold and also quite warm! The movement of the sun and her strength amaze us every year. She does rule up here. As, I guess, she does in all places.

OUR SUN

The true center of our world
is the sun I would say.
We orbit around it once a year
and rely on it for life every day.

The sun provides the energy
that keeps everything alive.
From warming the earth to growing the plants,
without it we couldn't survive.

But it also gives us other gifts
that can entertain as well as give relief.
Without the sun, we wouldn't have shade
or the delightful shadows we see.

Another joy we get from the sun
is an amazing show at night;
explosive activity from gases on the sun
brings us the incredible northern lights.

Have you ever watched the sunrise
and seen the colors change across the earth?
It is a sight everyone should see at least once,
teaching that every day is like a new birth.

The sun is incredible with the water,
reflecting the sky—oh so blue.
It shimmers like diamonds and tiny sailboats
and teases your imagination, too.

Yes, sunshine is a glorious thing
and oh so welcome a sight.
As our days get longer in the spring,
we slowly get more day than night.

The aspect of the sun does change,
which means more or less raw heat.
After winter, the sun slowly warms,
and in summer I often must retreat.

Every day does come to a close,
and the sun has an amazing final show.
It paints the sky with colors deep and rich.
Then the horizon it slowly dips below.

Yes, the sun is a needed and integral part
of our lives in so many ways.
It gives us life, food, and joy
and always starts a brand-new day.

Rainy Lake is a beautiful lake with so many wild and pristine places to explore—it could truly take a lifetime. It will grab your soul. This poem reflects a common day on Rainy.

Rainy Lake

Yesterday was a very good day.
I spent it on Rainy Lake.
The sun was shining, and the sky was blue.
I knew good memories we would make.

We rode in the boat for about an hour,
on our way to a favorite beach.
We saw eagles, pelicans, and lots of loons;
it was a dream that came within our reach.

When I'm out on the waters of Rainy Lake,
any stress simply disappears.
It's like there's a connection to my soul,
an experience that is truly premier.

The water can be so very blue,
whitecaps or smooth like glass.
It is so clear and refreshing to see
and provides memories that through time will last.

We walked the beach while collecting rocks
and picked up sticks from beaver chews.
The day was absolutely idyllic—
we enjoyed a stunning, full-of-islands view.

The clouds were few and far between,
teasing one's imagination with their shapes.
Trees stood tall along the horizon,
sort of framing this beautiful landscape.

Yes, it certainly was a very good day.
On Rainy Lake, you can't go wrong.
It grabs your heart and your soul
and makes a connection that is unbreakably strong.

As I continued to learn about the power of positive thought and manifesting your desires, my poems started including more aspects of life. Laughter and hugs and the oh-so-important personal relationships. These poems came out of me as I so wanted to share this wonderful knowledge of how everyone can create the life they want. Yes, life is good.

LIFE IS GOOD

Life is good on this earth,
as it is supposed to be.
Yet there is conflict of all kinds,
which helps us grow spiritually.

The tough times are no fun to endure
but do allow for important change.
If you look back on your times of growth,
did they not come out of some pain?

Change is one thing we can count on.
Growth and improvement are what we seek.
So when we get that icky feeling inside,
just realize that in itself it's a great technique.

Our thoughts create our feelings.
Our feelings are our greatest guide.
Our thoughts are something we can change,
which means we are in control of this ride.

So if we focus on how we feel,
being mindful of our thinking too,
we can create the lives we want
and to our own selves remain true.

AMAZING LIFE

In this amazing life on earth,
there's so much we can learn,
but I have found it comes down to
thoughts and feelings, our biggest concern.

Everything has its own energy,
and the vibrations never stop.
What we think and feel creates our life;
in that you can put great stock.

Wherever you put your thoughts
will bring that into your life.
So think about what it is you want,
not what will only bring you strife.

The power is in each one of us,
and life is supposed to be good.
It's a simple but different message,
one we ideally get in our childhood.

Learning the laws of the universe
means something very different to me now.
This knowledge is exciting to learn about
and share—the wonderful secret of the how.

Recognizing that we *can* change our thoughts
and do have amazing power inside
is thrilling wisdom to have faith in,
learning all the ways it can be applied.

To know your job is to feel good …
what an uplifting, empowering thought!
It'll change the way you look at life
and even the things that will be sought.

So focus on your feelings;
your thoughts they'll tell you about.
Lead with your heart. You can't go wrong,
and your life will be good, no doubt.

I have always been a hugger. It seems the natural way to greet someone. I have learned some people don't care for hugs—though most do. I have also learned that those who don't care for hugs often come around to where they love them. So I continue to hug. We hug in so many different ways and for so many different reasons ...

A HUG

One of the simple joys in life
is a hug—at least to me.
It sends a simple message
and will bring a smile—guaranteed.

A hug can be a show of affection,
a means to say hello or good-bye.
It can help you just to feel better
and is great when something makes you cry.

Hugs, I think, are quite healthy,
and an amazing thing I've found
is the more hugs you give away,
the more they return—like a rebound.

They help at those awkward moments
when you just don't know what to say.
Hugs give strong communication
and can truly help pick up one's day.

An interesting thing I've noticed
is that children learn to hug early on.
It's their natural reaction to a feeling of joy
and sends that feeling right back quite strong.

There are lots of different ways to hug,
from air hugs to light pats on the back.
From no body-touch to full bear hugs,
the different styles connect us—a fact.

So I encourage you to take the time
to hug those you love when you can.
It is good for hearts and souls and minds.
Make it a part of your daily plan.

Laughing brings such joy to me—I try to do it every day. It is a miraculous cure and just feels good.

Photo by Ron Meer

LAUGHTER

One of the things I enjoy in life
is a good laugh that comes from deep within.
It fills me with joy and is healthy too,
and so fun to share with a friend.

Isn't it great when you think of something
that makes you outright laugh again?
Or when you laugh so hard your muscles cramp
and you simply must stop that continual grin.

Remember when you were younger
and would laugh at times when you should not?
Like on a Sunday in the church pew,
or in class, where in trouble you got.

But laughing is something to do often.
You can't be sad and laugh at the same time.
Laughing increases your immunity and lowers your stress
and even increases the endorphins in your mind.

A good laugh can start a conversation
or break the ice and put someone at ease.
It's an excellent tool when teaching kids.
It makes people smile, which will always please.

I have a goal I try to live by
of having at least one belly laugh every day.
It's a great way for a day to start or end
and allows for quality time to play.

Laughing is something so worthwhile;
it is good for your well-being and health.
It can make you rich on the inside,
which is where you'll find true wealth.

I hope you have someone in your life
that is a laugh maker for you.
Mine makes me laugh so hard I cry …
and lose fluids elsewhere too.

These next few are about different parts of life—being a parent, aging, retiring …

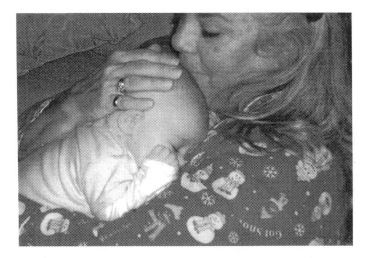

Photo by Ron Meer

CYCLES OF LIFE

Life has many different cycles
with amazements in each one.
There's much to learn along the way;
we're really never done.

I went through the parenting cycle,
truly loving being a mom.
Watching your children grow and change
is a truly satisfying phenomenon.

Your love is strong and especially deep;
you don't think it could ever be more.
Somehow those years do pass by
and leave wonderful memories to adore.

Your children do grow up and leave
to lead lives of their own.
That is the expectation we have,
another cycle in life—a cornerstone.

Then the next generation begins,
and an amazing thing happens inside.
You thought nothing could beat being a mom,
but a grandma? That does override.

Seeing a child of your child
is like seeing a cycle complete.
The joy it brings is hard to express;
the feeling is true, fulfilling, so sweet.

Then getting to know this grandchild
brings so much joy and love.
It makes sense of why things are as they are,
and it's what life's real moments are made of.

Seeing your child parenting their own
is both touching and humbling too.
You see your place in the cycles of life;
life goes on—words with great truth.

As life's cycles come and go,
try to embrace and enjoy each one.
They each have something for us to learn.
Yes, life is good and should be fun.

GROWING OLD

My grandmother was a great lady
and was the first to impress on me
the strange phenomenon of aging,
of which now I can clearly see.

I try to tell the younger folk
about this aging thing.
It sort of sneaks up on you;
you don't even know it's happening.

Then one day you look in the mirror
and are surprised by what you see.
You wonder how this could be true
and marvel at this reality.

Just when did those eyes drop?
And look at the lines on my face!
I see some wrinkles on my neck,
and silver hairs are commonplace!

Amazing as this may sound,
young is what I feel *inside*.
So when I look at the outer package,
I wonder, contemplate, and sigh.

For a long time, I felt and *was* young;
I don't think I ever entered middle age.
But somehow now I'm on the other side
and realize I have turned that page.

My flexibility has stiffened a bit.
My muscles are not quite as strong.
I'm not as fast as I used to be,
and I sometimes don't last as long.

But basically I'm a young person,
even though I don't look that way.
Yet I have the wisdom of my years
and the experience of life, I must say.

So remember as you live your life,
if you think age is the key,
this strange phenomenon of young in old
will soon, too, be your reality.

After working for many years, the time came to retire, or "graduate" as I called it. I thoroughly enjoyed my work and did many different, interesting, and exciting things. But I was ready for a change, a new chapter …

My New Chapter

As I start yet another chapter
in this story that I'm livin',
it's fun to look back and truly see
all the wonderful things I've been given.

We spend our lives learning our world
and figuring out how to fit in it.
The experiences and knowledge that we gain
form the tapestry of life that we knit.

It's interesting how society is structured,
and your work identifies who you are.
You climb the ladder year after year,
always striving to become a star.

We sometimes lose our focus,
and our work becomes the end, not the means.
The things that matter most in life
slip to the shadows, it seems.

One thing leads to another.
At the time, you often don't see.
There are reasons things happen as they do;
faith in this can set you free.

The time finally comes to graduate,
when you get to set your own time line.
It takes a while to change into that mode,
but the freedom it gives is divine.

You find the work goes on without you,
sometimes as though you were never there.
But the difference is *your* priorities have changed,
and things just look different everywhere.

So, another chapter has now begun,
one I happily enter into.
With excitement of new memories to make,
I look forward to this chapter with you.

As I continue to learn and marvel at what this world has to offer, the poems continue to arrive. It brings me great joy, and through the support and love of family and friends, I am at the point of sharing this with you. I hope a smile comes to your face and your heart.

ABOUT THE AUTHOR

Only when she changed the way she looked at the world did her world look different. In 2004 LeeAnn Meer became aware of the law of attraction, gratitude, mindfulness and intentionally living your life. While she has written poems for 50+ years, she now has poems that just come out about the new way she sees her world. LeeAnn continues to marvel at her world as she happily lives on Rainy Lake in northern Minnesota with her husband, Ron and dog, Tango.

Printed in the United States
By Bookmasters